BECOMING HIS

A 30-Day Journey to Intimacy with God

by
Rachel Jakam

Jathought Press

Allen, Texas

Paperback ISBN: 979-8-9996335-2-1

CONTENTS

HOW TO USE THIS DEVOTIONAL

Each day includes:

- A short Scripture passage
- A brief devotional reflection
- A closing prayer
- A prompt for journaling, meditation, or response

You can go through it:

- One day at a time, for 30 days
- One week at a time (e.g., five days a week for six weeks)
- Or at your own pace

Tip: Keep a journal or notebook nearby. You may want to write your prayers, your responses, or what God highlights as you reflect.

Don't aim to finish quickly.

Aim to draw near.

God is already here.

"To the one becoming. You are seen, held, and deeply loved."

INTRODUCTION

This devotional was born from the same journey shared in Becoming His, the book; a path from inherited faith to intimate freedom.

It's easy to know about God and still feel far from Him. But intimacy doesn't begin with knowing more. It begins with coming closer.

Somewhere in the space between striving and surrender, I discovered a truth that changed me: God isn't asking you to perform. He's inviting you to be present.

These 30 days are a quiet invitation. Not to fix everything. Not to prove anything. But to slow down, open your heart, and let Him speak.

Whether you're in a season of healing, longing for clarity, or simply learning to walk loved, this space is for you. God is already near, ready to meet you with Grace, truth, and unwavering love.

You'll also find something personal woven in a few simple recipes from my childhood. They are small tastes of home, tucked between these pages like warm memories. My hope is that they bring a little joy and comfort as you reflect and rest.

Let these pages be sacred space. A daily rhythm of stillness and honest conversation between you and the One who calls you His.

Part 1

ROOTED IN IDENTITY

Discovering who you are and whose you are

"Before I formed you in the womb I knew you, before you were born, I set you apart;

I appointed you as a prophet to the nations."

"Jeremiah 1:5"

Day 1: *Fully Known, Fully Loved*

We spend so much of life trying to be understood: explaining our hearts, justifying our actions, proving our worth. But long before anyone else laid eyes on you, God already knew you, completely, intimately, without condition. He didn't just accept you; He deliberately chose you in love.

Nathanael experienced this when Jesus said, "I saw you while you were still under the fig tree before Philip called you" (John 1:48). He was stunned to be seen in a hidden place, without introduction. To be seen, known, and loved without a mask; that's God's promise to you too.

Nothing in your past, your personality, your fears, or your failures takes Him by surprise. He sees the places you hide, the questions you carry, and still says: "You are Mine." You were woven together with intention, crafted for a purpose. Never an accident. Never too much or not enough.

Being fully known can feel frightening in a world that prefers filters. But with God, you don't need to perform. You are already seen. And deeply loved. The more you rest in His gaze, the more you discover freedom begins right there; in knowing you have nothing to prove.

Reflection Question — Where do I still feel the need to prove my worth?

Prayer — Father, thank You for seeing me fully and loving me still. Teach me to rest in the truth that I don't need to prove anything to belong to You.

"For He chose us in Him before the creation of the world to be holy and blameless in His sight. In love"

Ephesians 1:4

Day 2: *Already Chosen*

The human heart longs to be chosen, not for what it does, but for who it is. So often we live as if love must be earned, as if acceptance could vanish overnight. But God's love is not like the world love. It does not hinge on your performance or position.

Before your successes or failures, He already saw you and called you His. Not out of obligation, but desire. You are not merely tolerated, you are treasured.

Abraham was called before he proved his faith (Genesis 12). Jeremiah heard God say, "Before I formed you in the womb, I knew you" (Jeremiah 1:5). God always chooses first, long before we can prove our value.

In a world of comparison, this truth anchors you: you don't need to fight to be noticed or fear being forgotten. The Creator of the universe has already chosen you.

Maybe you wonder, "What if I fail tomorrow?" The good news is that your chosenness isn't fragile. It rests on His faithfulness, not yours. You were chosen before time began.

Reflection Question — How would my life look different if I truly believed I am already chosen?

Prayer — Lord, thank You that I am no accident. Help me live from Your choosing, not in the race for acceptance.

"Therefore, if anyone is in Christ, the new creation has come: The old has gone, the new is here!"

2 Corinthians 5:17

Day 3: *Not Who I Was*

God didn't just repair what was broken, He made you new.

In Christ, you're not a polished version of the old you. You are a new creation. Your past, your failures, your old labels no longer define you.

Paul is living proof. Once a persecutor of the church, he became an apostle to the nations. Believers at first doubted his conversion, it seemed too radical (Acts 9). But God had spoken a new name and a new calling over him.

What God did in Paul, He does in us. The old nature is crucified, and a new identity rises. You don't need to earn this new self; it has already been given to you.

Today, choose to walk as one already transformed. Your past is buried. New life is breathing within you.

Reflection Question — What part of my past am I still carrying even though God has already buried it?

Prayer — Jesus, thank You for making me new. Teach me not to live as if I were still the old me, but to walk in the freedom of my new identity.

"But you are a chosen people, a royal priesthood, a holy nation, God's special possession, that you may declare the praises of Him who called you out of darkness into His wonderful light."

1 Peter 2: 9

Day 4: *Trading Labels for Truth*

Even as a new creation, it's easy to carry old labels: "not enough," "failure," "forgotten," "too much." Those words don't define who you are, they're lies the enemy hopes you'll believe.

God calls you by your true name. You are chosen. Royal. Set apart. Not defined by your past or others' opinions, but by His living Word.

Think of Gideon. He saw himself as weak and insignificant, hiding from his enemies. Yet the angel of the Lord greeted him: "The Lord is with you, mighty warrior" (Judges 6:12). Where Gideon saw weakness, God already saw a deliverer.

Each day, you are invited to trade false labels for God's truth. The exchange may feel like a battle because old labels cling tightly. But every time you believe what He says about you, your posture and vision shift a little more toward freedom.

Reflection Question — What false label do I need to lay down today so I can put on God's truth?

Prayer — Father, help me let go of false identities I've carried too long. Teach me to believe and live from Your gaze: loved, chosen, treasured.

"My sheep listen to my voice; I know them, and they follow me."

John 10:27

Day 5: *God's Voice Over My Inner Critic*

There's a voice that feels familiar yet carries no love. It highlights your flaws, replays your failures, and whispers: "You'll never be enough." That voice is not God's.

His voice corrects without condemning. It calls you forward, not with shame but with truth. It leads with peace.

As a child, Samuel heard his name in the night. Three times he thought Eli was calling him (1 Samuel 3). But it wasn't the voice of man, it was the voice of God. That story reminds us how easily we confuse voices: our thoughts, our critics, the opinions of others. But when Samuel learned to answer, "Speak, Lord, for your servant is listening," he discovered God's voice always brings clarity and peace.

Your inner critic shouts loudly because it's familiar. But familiarity isn't truth. The more time you spend with your Shepherd, the easier it becomes to recognize His voice; the one that heals, restores, and strengthens.

Reflection Question — Which of my thoughts feel true but don't reflect the heart of God?

Prayer — Lord, help me hear and follow Your voice above every other, even my own. Silence the noise of shame and lead me in Your truth.

"Therefore, there is now no condemnation for those who are in Christ Jesus."

Romans 8:1

Day 6: *Shaped by Grace, Not Guilt*

Guilt says, "You've failed; hide."

Grace says, "You've failed; come close, I'll restore you."

Guilt often disguises itself as humility, but it's a heavy chain that paralyzes. Only grace sets free.

Remember the woman caught in adultery (John 8). Her accusers demanded justice; the law seemed clear. But Jesus sent them away in silence and spoke life instead: "Then neither do I condemn you. Go now and leave your life of sin." Grace lifted her where guilt would have crushed her.

God is not shaping your heart with shame but with His kindness. Even your stumbles can become steps toward restoration. Lift your eyes, you are not defined by failure but by His forgiveness.

Reflection Question — Where have I let guilt steer me instead of grace?

Prayer — Jesus, let me live as one forgiven, not hidden in shame. May Your grace reshape how I see myself and how I walk forward.

"You are my hiding place; You will protect me from trouble and surround me with songs of deliverance."

Psalm 32:7

Day 7: *Safe in His Presence*

You are surrounded, not by pressure or the demand to perform, but by His presence.

God doesn't just go before you; He covers your past and meets you in the present. His presence isn't a courtroom where you defend yourself. It's a home where you rest.

David sang, "You are my hiding place; you will protect me from trouble and surround me with songs of deliverance" (Psalm 32:7). He knew fear, failure, and shame, but he also discovered that God Himself was his refuge. That promise is yours too.

You don't need polished prayers or hidden pain. You can come as you are. Even now, He says: "In My presence, you are safe." And the more you dwell there, the more you realize this refuge isn't temporary it's eternal.

Reflection Question — What would I say to God today if I truly believed His presence is my safe place?

Prayer — Father, help me stop hiding from You. Teach me to rest in the safety of Your presence, without pretending.

<u>Recipe</u>: Plantain & Scramble Eggs

INGREDIENTS

2 ripe plantains (yellow with black spots)

1 tbsp oil

4 eggs

1/2 small onion, chopped

Salt and pepper to taste

Yield: 2-3

Prep Time: 5 MIN

Total Time: 10 MIN

Growing up, plantain and scrambled eggs were more than just food; they were comfort, warmth, and love on a plate. I remember waking up to the sound of oil crackling in the pan and the sweet smell of ripe plantains caramelizing.

To this day, every time I fry plantains and scramble eggs, I feel like I'm back in that kitchen; barefoot, hungry, and happy.

Just as golden plantains and scrambled eggs once brought warmth and comfort to the home, so the presence of God reminds us that we are always safe with Him. Food may nourish the body, but His presence nourishes the soul and brings rest to the weary heart.

DIRECTIONS

Peel and slice plantains; fry in oil until golden (3–4 minutes per side). Set aside.

Sauté onions in the same pan for 2 minutes.

Beat and season eggs, scramble until cooked.

Serve with fried plantains.

WEEKLY REFLECTION

- o What did God show me this week?
- o What truth challenged me most?
- o What am I praying for as I continue?

_____

_____

_____

_____

_____

_____

_____

_____

_____

_____

_____

_____

_____

_____

_____

_____

Part 2

HEALING THE HEART

Letting God tend to the wounds we've carried too long.

"The Lord is close to the brokenhearted and saves those who are crushed in spirit."

Psalm 34: 18

Day 8: *When the Past Isn't Over*

Sometimes you move forward, take on new responsibilities, even smile again… until one memory, one word, one encounter reopens the wound you thought was healed. You wonder: "Why does this still hurt?"

It isn't weakness. Healing is rarely a straight line. Time alone doesn't erase everything. Sometimes God allows old pain to resurface; not to shame you, but to touch it more deeply with His hand.

Even Jeremiah admitted, "I well remember them, and my soul is downcast within me" (Lamentations 3:20). Yet in that confession he also discovered hope.

You don't need to hide your hurt or pretend you've fully overcome. God doesn't ask for a perfect version of you. He draws near to your heart as it is; scars, sensitivities, and all. His arms are wide enough for your memories and your tears.

Stop running. Hand Him that part of your story. It's not regression, it's an invitation to deeper healing.

Reflection Question — What old wound do I need to place in God's hands today?

Prayer   Lord, I bring You what still aches. Thank You for being close to the brokenhearted. Step into my memories and bring healing where time has not been enough.

"I remember my affliction and my wandering, the bitterness and the gall. I well remember them, and my soul is downcast within me. Yet this I call to mind and therefore I have hope."

Lamentations 3:19-21

Day 9: *Naming the Wound*

Avoiding pain never heals it. Naming it opens the door to light.

Jeremiah didn't hide his grief he wrote it, prayed it, confessed it (Lamentations 3). That honesty became the doorway through which hope entered.

As long as wounds remain silent, they keep power in the dark. But when you dare to say, "That hurt me," you stop carrying it alone. You give space for the Great Healer to enter.

David prayed, "Record my misery; list my tears on your scroll, are they not in your record?" (Psalm 56:8). Naming the pain was his way of refusing to let it have the last word.

Your broken words don't scare God. They make room for His comfort to land.

Reflection Question — What wound have I kept silent that God is inviting me to name?

Prayer — Lord, give me courage to name my pain honestly. Step into the places I confess, and turn them into seeds of hope.

"Record my misery; list my tears on your scroll— are they not in your record?"

Psalm 56:8

Day 10: *Permission to Grieve*

Tears are not weakness, nor a lack of faith. They are sacred space where heaven bends close.

Our culture tells us to "move on quickly," as if tears should be hidden. But God treasures every one of your cries. "Record my misery; list my tears on your scroll, are they not in your record?" (Psalm 56:8). They rise as silent prayers before Him.

Jesus Himself wept at Lazarus's tomb (John 11:35). If the Son of God let His tears flow, how much more can you release yours without shame? Your tears are not an ending but a passageway, a path toward comfort.

So, if your heart feels heavy today, don't be afraid to weep. Lay your tears at the Father's feet. They water the soil where His hope can grow.

Reflection Question — What loss do I need to grieve before God without shame?

Prayer — Jesus, I bring You my tears as a language only You fully understand. Meet me in my sorrow, and turn my weeping into hope.

"He heals the brokenhearted and binds up their wounds."

Psalm 147:3

Day 11: *Inviting God into the Pain*

Pain tends to isolate. We sometimes believe God only wants our strength and victories. But healing begins when you open your darkest places and whisper, "Lord, come here."

He doesn't wait for perfect words or polished prayers. He meets you in raw honesty: "This hurts."

Even Jesus, in Gethsemane, didn't hide His anguish. He prayed with intensity, and an angel came to strengthen Him (Luke 22:43). The place of suffering became the place of encounter. Often, it's in our most vulnerable cries that God's presence feels the most tangible.

Your pain can become a sanctuary where His faithfulness shows up. You don't have to sit in the dark alone; God sits with you and reminds you: "You are not abandoned."

Reflection Question — Where am I still keeping God at a distance in my suffering?

Prayer — Father, I invite You into the places I've hidden. Bring Your love and turn what feels heavy into testimony of Your faithfulness.

"Blessed are those who mourn, for they will be comforted."

Mathew 5:4

Day 12: *You Are Not Too Much*

Maybe someone once told you: "You're too emotional. Too intense. Too sensitive." Over time, you believed it. You learned to shrink your heart, fearing that your depth was a problem.

But Jesus says the opposite. "Blessed are those who mourn, for they will be comforted" (Matthew 5:4). Your emotions are not a burden to Him, they are places where His comfort meets you.

Mary of Bethany wept and poured out perfume at Jesus' feet (John 12). Many judged her as excessive. But Jesus saw her act as beautiful worship. What others considered "too much," He received as treasure.

Your sensitivity is not weakness; it's a doorway for God's love. Your tears may encourage someone else. Your depth may open a path for others to express what they've been afraid to show. What you think is "too much" may be exactly where God wants to reveal Himself.

Reflection Question — What emotion I've hidden in shame does God want to receive today as worship?

Prayer — Lord, thank You for welcoming me as I am. Help me see my sensitivity not as a burden, but as a gift You use to reflect Your heart.

"Being confident of this, that he who began a good work in you will carry it on to completion until the day of Christ Jesus."

Philippians 1:6

Day 13: *Your Story isn't Over*

Your past does not define your destination. Too often we treat failure like a period. But God sees it as a comma, part of a story He's still writing.

Paul is proof. Once a persecutor of Christians, he became an apostle. If God hadn't spoken the final word, Paul's story would have ended in hatred. Instead, grace rewrote it.

Moses too thought his calling was finished after fleeing Egypt. Yet decades later, God called him from a desert to deliver His people. What Moses saw as failure, God used as preparation.

The shame that tries to keep you bound to who you were is not your author. God is.

God doesn't abandon His projects. Your life is not unfinished; it's in progress. What you thought was an ending may be the beginning of another chapter. You are a living story still unfolding.

Reflection Question — What part of my story do I need to see with God's eyes—as work still in progress?

Prayer — Lord, I give You the chapters I thought were broken or closed. Thank You for continuing Your good work in me. Help me walk with confidence, knowing You always have the last word.

"I will give you a new heart and put a new spirit in you; I will remove from you your heart of stone and give you a heart of flesh."

Ezekiel 36:26

Day 14: *Soft Heart, Strong Spirit*

When life wounds us, it's tempting to harden. Hardness feels protective, if nothing gets in, nothing can break me. But a hard heart also blocks joy, love, and healing.

God doesn't call you to grow harder. He invites you to stay tender under His care. "I will give you a new heart... I will remove from you your heart of stone and give you a heart of flesh" (Ezekiel 36:26).

Jesus modeled this perfectly: gentle and humble in heart, yet strong enough to carry the cross. His compassion wasn't weakness; it was power poured out in sacrifice.

Keeping a tender heart isn't naïve; it's courageous. It means staying open to love, trust, and healing even when life gives reasons to close. That tenderness reflects God's own heart, a strength no wound can destroy.

Reflection Question — What part of me have I hardened to protect myself? Am I willing to let God soften it?

Prayer — Lord, take the places where I've grown hard and make them tender again. I want to feel, love, and live fully without fear.

Recipe: Cameroonian-style Fried Rice ("Riz Sauté") with Dried Fish

INGREDIENTS

Yield: 4-5

2.5 cup (500g) of rice

5 smoked herring

6 large fresh tomatoes

1 leek, 1 stalk of celery

1 clove of garlic, 2 onions

Salt, pepper

5 Tbsp oil

1 small chili pepper (optional)

Prep Time: 15 MIN

Total Time: 40 MIN

In many Cameroonian homes, "riz sauté" is more than just fried rice; it's a celebration of creativity, and community. I remember visiting my grandmother in the village during school holidays. She always kept some dried fish in the kitchen, soaking up the smoky flavor of firewood cooking.

This dish reminds me of those carefree days and the love tucked into every spoonful.

The fragrance of fried rice, shared around the family table, points to the healing that often begins in the simple moments of meals and togetherness. In the same way, God restores our wounded hearts and invites us to share His comfort like an abundant feast that satisfies many.

DIRECTIONS

Wash and drain the rice; set it aside. Clean the smoked fish by removing skin, bones, and head.

Finely chop or blend the leek, chili, celery, bell pepper, onion, tomatoes, and garlic, then sauté them in hot oil with the cleaned fish for 5 minutes. Add the rice, stir well for another 5 minutes, then season with salt, pepper.

Pour in water, cover, and cook on low heat for about 30 minutes, adding a little water as needed until the rice is fully cooked and liquid absorbed. Gently mix in the fish, cook for 3–5 more minutes. Serve hot with pepper sauce and ripe plantains.

WEEKLY REFLECTION

- o What did God show me this week?
- o What truth challenged me most?
- o What am I praying for as I continue?

_____

_____

_____

_____

_____

_____

_____

_____

_____

_____

_____

_____

_____

_____

_____

_____

Part 3

FORGIVENESS & FREEDOM

*Letting go of the past to live
fully in the present.*

"Come to me, all you who are weary and burdened, and I will give you rest."

Matthew 11:28

Day 15: *Rest for the Pressured Heart*

We don't always realize how much we're carrying… until the moment we finally lay it down. Expectations. Invisible responsibilities. Guilt over "not enough." Fear of "falling behind." All of it weighs heavy.

But Jesus says: "Come to me, all you who are weary and burdened, and I will give you rest" (Matthew 11:28). Rest is not a reward for the strong; it's a gift for the tired.

Elijah once reached the point of despair, even asking God to take his life. Before God spoke to him, He gave Elijah food and water (1 Kings 19). Sometimes our souls need simple rest before they can hear more.

His rest reminds you; you are not God, and you don't have to be. You are invited to lay it down. You were designed to lay it down.

Reflection Question — What burden am I carrying that Jesus never asked me to carry?

Prayer — Jesus, I bring You the weight I feel. I receive Your invitation to rest and trust You with what I cannot carry.

"For if you forgive other people when they sin against you, your heavenly Father will also forgive you."

Matthew 6: 14

Day 16: *Obedience Before Emotion*

Forgiveness is not a feeling you wait for; it's a decision you choose.

If you wait until you feel like forgiving, you may wait a lifetime. Jesus, on the cross, prayed: "Father, forgive them" (Luke 23:34) while the pain was still raw. That was not sentiment, it was obedience and love.

Forgiving doesn't minimize the hurt. It places the debt in God's hands. It declares: "This offense is real, but it will not rule my heart."

Feelings may take time to catch up, but heaven honors the choice to obey before you feel it.

And when you obey, even with trembling hands; God meets you there. He softens what's hard. He strengthens what's weak. And, He brings peace where there was once only pain.

You don't have to feel it to begin. You just have to say yes.

Reflection Question — What concrete decision of forgiveness can I make today, even if I don't feel it yet?

Prayer — Father, I won't wait for my emotions to give me permission to obey. I choose to forgive by faith, trusting Your grace to carry me.

"Bear with each other and forgive one another... Forgive as the Lord forgave you."

Colossians 3: 13

Day 17: *Forgiving to Be Free*

Some wounds are forgiven in one step. Others require layers. You forgive once, and then the pain resurfaces and you forgive again. That isn't failure; it's the normal process of healing.

Peter asked Jesus how many times he should forgive. Jesus replied, "Not seven times, but seventy-seven times" (Matthew 18:22). In other words, keep forgiving.

Each time you release, you breathe freer. Each time you resist bitterness, another chain breaks. Forgiveness isn't weakness; it's perseverance that leads to freedom.

Freedom doesn't always come from one heroic moment but from repeated, faithful releasing. And step by step, your heart unravels from the grip of resentment.

God sees your repeated yes. He honors your consistency, not your perfection. And each time you choose Grace again, the weight gets lighter, and your heart grows freer

Reflection Question — Who or what do I need to forgive again today so I can keep moving in freedom?

Prayer — Jesus, give me strength to keep forgiving, even when the hurt resurfaces. I choose to release again until Your healing is complete in me.

"... Do not grieve, for the joy of the Lord is your strength."

Nehemiah 8:10

Day 18: *Joy is Resistance*

Joy doesn't ignore reality; it transforms it. Choosing joy in the middle of hardship is declaring that sorrow will not have the last word.

Nehemiah told the grieving people: "Do not grieve, for the joy of the Lord is your strength" (Nehemiah 8:10). Their joy was not in circumstances but in God.

Paul and Silas sang in prison, beaten and chained (Acts 16). Their worship became a weapon, opening doors and breaking chains. Their joy wasn't denial. It was strength that shook the darkness.

You are free to laugh again. To love again. To hope again. Joy is your act of resistance against despair.

Reflection Question — Where can I choose joy today as strength, not denial?

Prayer — God, restore to me the joy that lifts my eyes and strengthens my heart. Let joy be my song, even in the valley.

"Do not take revenge, my dear friends, but leave room for God's wrath, for it is written: 'It is mine to avenge; I will repay,' says the Lord."

Romans 12:19

Day 19: *Trusting God with Justice*

There's a deep desire in us to fix what's wrong—defend ourselves, make things right, demand justice. But God calls us to let go: "It is mine to avenge; I will repay" (Romans 12:19).

David could have killed Saul in the cave (1 Samuel 24). Instead, he refused, trusting God to judge. That choice kept him free from bitterness and regret.

Letting go of vengeance doesn't deny the wrong; it refuses to let resentment chain your heart. God sees. God knows. God does not forget.

Justice matters to God more than it ever could to us. He sees. He knows. He will not overlook what was done. But He also sees you and He wants to protect your peace while He handles the rest.

When you entrust justice to Him, you make space for Him to defend your cause and protect your peace.

Reflection Question — What would it look like in my relationships to entrust justice to God?

Prayer — Lord, I release my need to make things right on my own. I trust You with justice and choose peace over revenge.

"He has made everything beautiful in its time..."

Ecclesiastes 3:11

Day 20: *Releasing the Timeline*

Waiting can be one of faith's hardest tests. You pray, you hope, you move forward… yet nothing seems to change. You grip the calendar, desperate for God to match your timing.

But delays are not denials. God's timing is not punishment, it's preparation. What feels like delay may be unseen orchestration, work within you that you could never do alone.

Abraham and Sarah waited years before Isaac was born. Their tears and doubts didn't cancel God's promise. He wasn't late, He was right on time.

Imagine holding your own calendar, counting the days with anxious fingers. God invites you to open it, hand it over, and let Him write with you. His timing may not match yours, but it is always perfect.

Surrendering the timeline doesn't mean giving up. It means opening your hands. It means trading anxiety for peace. Because He is making it beautiful, even if you can't see it yet.

Reflection Question — What area of my life do I need to place in God's perfect timing today?

Prayer — Lord, I release my calendar and my expectations. Teach me to trust Your timing, even when I don't understand.

"When hard pressed, I cried to the Lord; He brought me into a spacious place."

Psalm 118: 5

Day 21: *Freedom on the Other Side*

God doesn't just want you to survive your struggles—He wants to bring you into freedom.

The psalmist declared: "When hard pressed, I cried to the Lord; he brought me into a spacious place" (Psalm 118:5). Freedom isn't abstract—it's the breath of a soul released from shame.

Picture a river: on one side, your pain and fear; on the other, the space God has promised. Many stands with one foot on each bank, but to cross you must let go. The water may be cold at first, but the other side holds peace, lightness, and joy.

Freedom is a choice. You can stay on the familiar shore, or you can trust God and step across.

There's freedom waiting. Not just eventually, but now. On the other side of surrender is a wide, open space where shame doesn't chase you, and fear no longer drives you. That's what He wants for you.

And that's where He's leading you, if you'll let go.

Reflection Question — What chain do I need to leave behind so I can step into freedom?

Prayer — Father, I loosen my grip and step forward. Lead me across to the freedom where my heart can breathe again.

Recipe: Hibiscus drink "Folere"

INGREDIENTS

Yield: 4-5

1 cup dried hibiscus petals

Prep Time: 5 MIN

4 cups water

Total Time: 15 MIN

Honey or sugar to taste

Optional: ginger, cloves, 1/2 cup pineapple or orange juice, extract of your choice (choose any to your taste)

As a child growing up in Cameroon, the deep red color of hibiscus drink—locally called foléré, bissap, or zobo in different parts of Africa; was always a sign of something special. It wasn't just a beverage; it was a celebration in a cup. Whether it was during holidays, weddings, or just a hot afternoon after school, a chilled glass of hibiscus drink brought joy and refreshment to everyone around.

Today, every time I make it, I'm reminded that the simplest ingredients; when made with love, carry the richest memories.

This bright and colorful drink reminds us of the freshness and freedom that come after a long season of heat and thirst. In the same way, the freedom found in Christ refreshes our weary hearts and opens a new space where we can finally breathe deeply again.

DIRECTIONS

Boil hibiscus with water and spices for 10 minutes.

Cool, strain, and stir in sweetener. Add any extract of your choice and juice if you want.

Chill and serve over ice.

WEEKLY REFLECTION

- o   What did God show me this week?
- o   What truth challenged me most?
- o   What am I praying for as I continue?

_____

_____

_____

_____

_____

_____

_____

_____

_____

_____

_____

_____

_____

_____

_____

Part 4

ABIDING & BECOMING

Growing deeper roots and bearing fruit that lasts.

"I am the vine; you are the branches. If you remain in me and I in you, you will bear much fruit..."

John 15:5

Day 22: *Remaining in Him*

It's not always the big, dramatic spiritual moments that grow us. More often, it's the quiet discipline of staying in His presence.

Jesus didn't call us to exhaust ourselves producing fruit. He simply said: "Remain in me." Transformation happens there. Strength renews there. Fruit is born there.

Abiding isn't perfection; it's returning again and again. In the middle of a packed schedule. In the ordinary spaces of daily life. In the high moments of faith and in the silence when you feel nothing at all.

Abiding looks like whispering a prayer while washing dishes. Opening Scripture instead of scrolling your phone. Letting go of control to simply be with Him.

You weren't made to live detached. You were created to remain in His love, in His presence, in His life.

Reflection Question — What practices help me stay close to Jesus throughout the day?

Prayer — Jesus, teach me to abide in You today. Help me return to You again and again, staying close, listening, and obeying.

"...but whose delight is in the law of the Lord... That person is like a tree planted by streams of water, which yields its fruit in season..."

Psalm 1: 2-3

Day 23: *Anchored by Rhythm*

Some days, your heart leaps with passion. Other days, it drags like a weary shadow. That's why you need rhythm; a steady anchor when emotions rise and fall.

Faith wasn't meant to run only on inspiration but to be rooted. Scripture, prayer, stillness, a whispered song in the morning or a verse at night; these aren't rules to check off. They are anchors for your soul.

God meets us in these steady, repeated gestures. You may not always see fruit right away, but roots planted deep by water will eventually bear harvest. Faithful rhythm may be quieter than grand bursts of zeal, but it is far more enduring.

You don't need to chase a mountaintop moment to grow in faith. You just need to show up, again and again. Let your rhythm become your resting place.

Reflection Question — What spiritual rhythm do I need to begin or return to?

Prayer — Lord, help me choose rhythm over striving. May my time with You be the root that steadies me even when I feel weak.

"After the earthquake came a fire, but the lord was not in the fire. And after the fire came a gentle whisper."

1 Kings 19:12

Day 24: *Listening for the whisper*

God doesn't always speak in the spectacular. Sometimes His voice comes as a whisper, soft enough to miss if we aren't still.

Elijah looked for God in the wind, the earthquake, the fire, but the Lord wasn't there. It was in the gentle whisper that His presence was known.

Our world is noisy. Notifications, news, endless demands. It's easy to miss the quiet voice of God. But His whisper still speaks, waiting for us to turn down the volume and listen.

Often, He speaks through peace that surpasses understanding, through a verse that won't leave your heart, through a quiet assurance: "You are not alone. I am here."

Today, make space. Lower the volume. Offer God silence. Listen for His whisper.

Reflection Question — Where do I need to lower the noise so I can hear God's voice?

Prayer — Lord, quiet the noise around me and within me. Train my heart to recognize Your gentle whisper.

"Though the fig tree does not bud… yet I will rejoice in the Lord, I will be joyful in God my Savior"

Habakkuk 3:17–18

Day 25: *Worship in the Valley*

It's easy to worship when life is blooming and prayers are answered quickly. But worship takes on its deepest meaning in the valley; when the ground feels dry, the sky feels silent, and the fruit hasn't come yet.

To worship in those moments isn't denial; it's declaration. It says: God is still good. His character hasn't changed. He is faithful. He is worthy.

Your worship doesn't have to be loud or polished. It can be a tired sigh, a hand lifted in the dark, a whispered "You are worthy" through tears. It is a hum of faith, a breath of surrender. Worship isn't about volume, it's about presence. And God always shows up when we offer Him our hearts. Every time you worship in the valley, you declare that your hope rests not in circumstances, but in Christ.

When you worship in the dark, heaven leans in. Chains begin to loosen. Not always around you, but definitely within you.

Reflection Question — What does worship look like in my current season?

Prayer — God, I choose to worship even here, even now. Not because life is perfect, but because You are faithful.

"Let this be written for a future generation, that a people not yet created may praise the Lord."

Psalm 102: 18

Day 26: *Writing with God*

Writing can be a sacred act. Not just documentation, but There's something holy about putting pen to paper. When you write with God, you're not just journaling, you're building an altar. A place where truth is remembered, tears are recorded, and hope is planted.

Writing can be a sacred act laying your story before God, building an altar of words. On the page, your prayers take form, your tears find space, your gratitude becomes memory.

Sometimes writing lightens the weight of pain. Other times, it opens your ears to hear God more clearly. A journal can become a hidden sanctuary, where ordinary life becomes divine conversation.

You don't need perfect words. Honesty is enough. Write your questions, victories, burdens. Invite God into your lines. One day, those words may guide you again or even testify to someone else of His faithfulness. It will be a record of His faithfulness. A testimony in ink.

So today, let your heart speak on paper. Write with Him, not just about Him.

Reflection Question — What do I need to write today as offering, cry, or declaration?

Prayer — Lord, teach me to write with You. Let my words reflect Your truth and remind me of who You've always been.

"Let us not become weary in doing good, for at the proper time we will reap a harvest if we do not give up."

Galatians 6:9

Day 27: *Faithfulness Over Flash*

Steadfastness rarely makes headlines. It isn't flashy. It looks like whispered prayers, repeated faithfulness, choices no one else sees, but God does.

The world applauds fast results and visible performance. But God delights in steady perseverance, the hidden yes in the secret place, the quiet choice to keep going. Like a gardener watering dry ground day after day, you remain faithful, and heaven notices.

Noah built an ark for years without a drop of rain, mocked by many. His persistence saved his family. Your quiet constancy, too, is seen by God.

Fruit doesn't depend on your speed but on His timing. Roots grow in the unseen before fruit shows in the open. Your steadfastness is not wasted it's seed in God's hands.

Reflection Question — Where is God asking me to keep going even when I'm weary?

Prayer — Lord, strengthen my hands and steady my heart. Help me trust Your timing as I keep sowing faithfully.

"Being confident of this, that He who began a good work in you will carry it on to completion until the day of Christ Jesus."

Philippians 1: 6

Day 28: *Still Becoming*

You don't need to have arrived to be on the right path. Becoming isn't failure, it's proof that God is still at work in you.

Picture a house under construction. The walls may be up, but the roof isn't finished. It's already a house, but still in progress. Your life is like that. Some days, progress is visible. Other days, it feels hidden. But the Architect hasn't stopped building.

Peter was still becoming. Impulsive and fragile, he denied Jesus. Yet God restored him and made him a rock of the church. His failures became part of his formation.

Every stage, even incomplete, belongs to His plan. You are not who you were yesterday, and you are not yet who you will be tomorrow. Most of all, you are His today, and that is enough.

Reflection **Question — Where can I give myself permission to be "in process"** instead of demanding perfection?

Prayer — Jesus, thank You that I'm not behind, I'm becoming. Help me see my growth through Your eyes, trusting You to finish what You started.

Recipe: Peanut Butter Soup

INGREDIENTS

Yield: 4-6

1.5 – 2 lbs. meat of your choice

Prep Time: 10 MIN

1 small onion, chopped

Total Time: 45 MIN

2 garlic cloves, minced

1-inch ginger root, grated

1/2 tsp white or black pepper

Hot pepper (optional)

Salt to taste

1/2 to 2/3 cup natural peanut butter (unsweetened, creamy)

4 cups water (or enough to cover meat and adjust consistency)

Peanut butter soup was a staple in our home, rich, comforting, and full of flavor. My mother made it with love, stirring stories into every pot as the aroma filled the house. We'd gather around the table with rice or fufu, sharing laughter and warmth with each bite. Even now, one taste brings me back to those sweet, simple moments of togetherness.

Best enjoyed with rice, plantain or yucca.

Rich and nourishing, peanut sauce symbolizes the constancy of love that never runs out. In the same way, God's faithfulness remains day after day sometimes quiet, sometimes deep, but always sufficient to sustain our becoming.

DIRECTIONS

Place the meat in a large pot. Add onions, garlic, ginger, pepper, and salt. Add just enough water to cover the meat. Boil for 15–20 minutes until the meat is partially cooked and infused with flavor.

In a bowl, mix the peanut butter with warm water until smooth. Pour the peanut mixture into the pot with the meat. Stir well to combine everything. Simmer uncovered on low heat for 20–25 min. Stir occasionally to prevent sticking. The soup will thicken and the oil will rise slightly to the top; that's a sign it's ready! Adjust salt and pepper to taste.

WEEKLY REFLECTION

o   What did God show me this week?

o   What truth challenged me most?

o   What am I praying for as I continue?

_____

_____

_____

_____

_____

_____

_____

_____

_____

_____

_____

_____

_____

_____

_____

_____

Part 5

LEGACY OF LOVE

*You're not just being healed;
you're being prepared to
carry healing.*

"I am reminded of your sincere faith, which first lived in your grandmother Lois and in your mother Eunice and, I am persuaded, now lives in you also."

2 Timothy 1:5

Day 29: *Healing That Flows Through You*

What God restores in you is never meant to stop with you. Healing always overflows, like a spring watering everything around it.

The chains you break today: fear, anger, shame, clear a new path for others. You may not have chosen the wounds of your family history, but you can choose what you pass on. Every forgiveness, every step into truth, every "yes" to God becomes a ripple reaching generations.

Timothy carried a living faith passed down from his mother and grandmother. Their faith became his inheritance. In the same way, your choices today can become tomorrow's testimony. A small act of faith now may be the answered prayer of a future generation.

God is not only working in you; He is working through you. Your healed story may one day become someone else's hope.

Reflection Question — What choice of healing I make today could become tomorrow's legacy?

Prayer — Lord, thank You for turning my healing into a testimony that blesses beyond me. Let my obedience open paths of freedom for my family, my community, and generations to come.

"As the Father has loved me, so have I loved you. Now remain in my love."

John 15:9

Day 30: *Living Loved, Living Free*

You don't have to chase God's love; it is already your starting place. The Father's love isn't a prize to earn; it's the foundation you live from. When you know you're loved, you breathe differently, walk differently, choose differently.

True freedom comes when you stop begging for what's already yours and start living in it. Freedom isn't the absence of limits; it's the assurance of His love that breaks the chains of fear and striving.

Jesus told His disciples: "As the Father has loved me, so have I loved you. Now remain in my love" (John 15:9). That love is not only your refuge; it is also your sending place. As you remain, you carry that love into your relationships, your words, your everyday life.

As you step out of these 30 days, hold onto this truth: You are deeply loved. You are already free. Your becoming isn't finished, but you can live rooted in His love today and give it away tomorrow.

Reflection Question — What does it look like to "walk in love" in the season ahead?

Prayer — Jesus, help me live as one who is already loved. Let that truth shape my thoughts, words, and ways of loving others. Thank You that You will never let me go.

Recipe: Banana Puff – Puff (Beignets)

INGREDIENTS

Yield: 4-5

3 ripe bananas, mashed

Prep Time: 10 MIN

1 cup corn flour or corn meal

Total Time: 25 MIN

1 cup all-purpose flour

Banana beignets were the ultimate childhood treat; crispy on the outside, soft and sweet on the inside. My mom will make then on the weekend and we'd sit on the porch with oily fingers and full mouths, laughing.

2 Tbsp. of sugar (optional)

1 tsp baking powder

1/2 tsp salt

Oil for deep frying

To this day, making banana beignets feels like pressing pause on the world and tasting a piece of home.

These crispy weekend treats remind us that life with God is not just about enduring, but about savoring. To live loved and free is to discover that His joy overflows into the smallest things, and that His love makes everything more delightful.

DIRECTIONS

Mash the bananas in a large bowl until smooth. Add sugar, salt, baking powder, cornmeal, and wheat flour to the mashed bananas. Mix well until you get a thick, sticky batter. If the batter is too loose, add a little more flour.

Heat oil in a deep pan over medium heat. Scoop spoonful of batter and carefully drop into the hot oil. Fry in batches, turning occasionally, until golden brown on all sides (about 5–7 minutes). Remove and drain on paper towels. Serve warm, plain or with a sprinkle of powdered sugar or a side of spicy pepper sauce.

WEEKLY REFLECTION

o   What did God show me this week?

o   What truth challenged me most?

o   What am I praying for as I continue?

_____

_____

_____

_____

_____

_____

_____

_____

_____

_____

_____

_____

_____

_____

_____

_____

CONCLUSION

This devotional is not the finish line; it's only the beginning. God's invitation to intimacy, healing, and transformation continues day after day.

If these pages have touched your heart, remember: there is always more. More grace to receive. More depth to enter. More love to be embraced by. And you are not walking this road alone. The Lord Himself walks with you, step by step, and He places companions along the way to lift you up.

Keep opening your heart to Him. Keep nurturing the daily rhythm of His presence. Write down your discoveries, sing your prayers, share your story. Every small step matter; it builds a legacy for you and for those who will follow after you.

And never forget: you don't need to have reached the end to know you are on the right path. You are already becoming loved, free, and rooted in Him. The One who began a good work in you will be faithful to bring it to completion.

CLOSING PRAYER

Lord, thank You for walking with me these past 30 days (or more). Thank You for the truths You've revealed, the lies You've unraveled, and the love You've poured into my heart.

Help me carry what I've learned, not just in my mind, but in how I live and love. Make me bold in obedience. Gentle in Grace. Rooted in truth.

I may not have all the answers, but I trust You only, the One who leads right. I am Yours. And I will keep becoming the person You had in mind when You formed me.

In Jesus' name.

Amen.

NOTES

(To use for your personal notes)

_____

_____

_____

_____

_____

_____

_____

_____

_____

_____

_____

_____

_____

_____

_____

_____

_____

_____

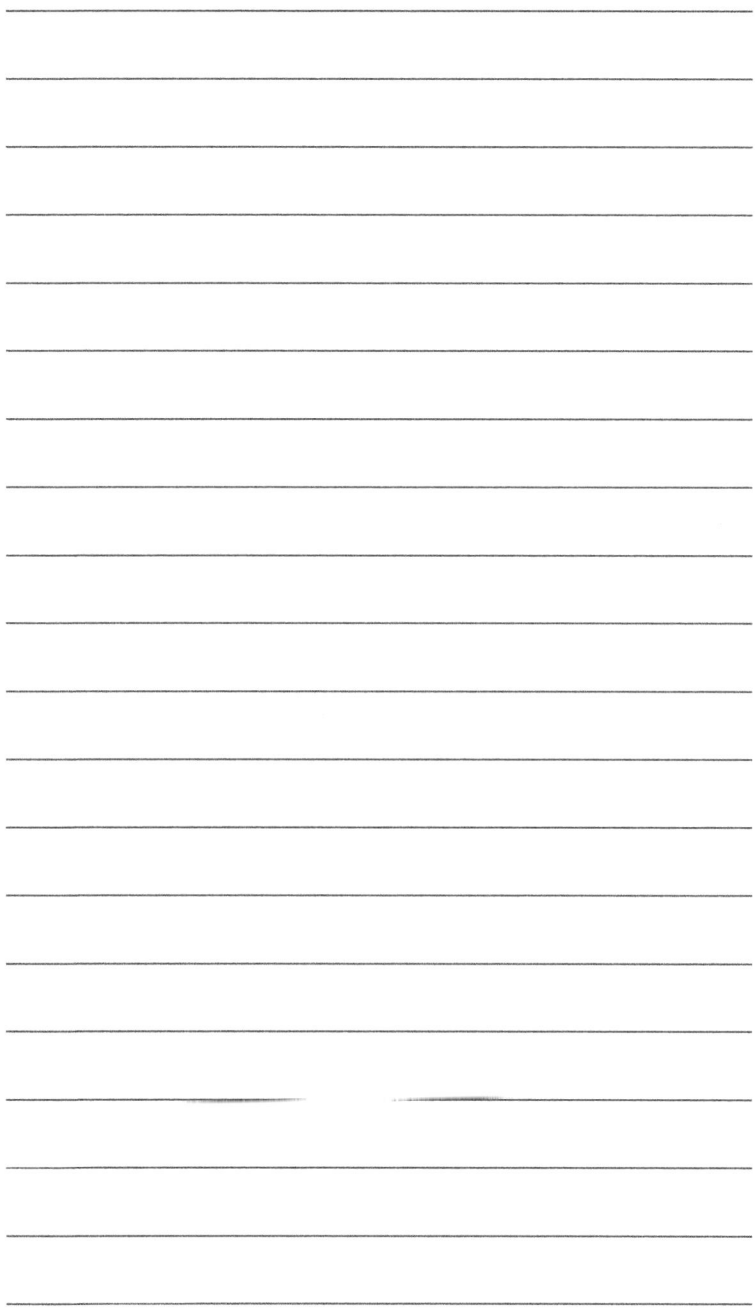

KEEP BECOMING

This devotional is just the beginning.

God's invitation to intimacy, healing, and transformation continues, one step at a time.

If this journey spoke to your heart, there's more waiting for you:

Read the full story in **Becoming His**, a personal testimony of surrender, restoration, and walking in identity.

Go deeper with the FREE **Becoming His 28-Day Companion Journal**, a space for Scripture reflection, prayer, and honest growth.

More on Becoming His: https://jathought.org/becoming-his/

Visit the blog at www.jathought.org

You'll find new posts, Scripture resources, and ways to stay connected to the journey.

You're not becoming alone.

He's with you in every step.

ABOUT THE AUTHOR

Rachel Jakam is a wife, mother, and finance professional with a heart for restoration and discipleship. Born into a legacy of Christian faith in Cameroon, Rachel's journey took a transformative turn when she moved from religious performance to a deeply personal walk with God.

She is the author of Becoming His, a memoir that invites readers to exchange striving for surrender and step into true intimacy with Christ. Through her writing, mentoring, and nonprofit work, Rachel walks alongside women navigating identity, healing, and spiritual growth.

Rachel is also the co-founder of EduExcel Foundation, a nonprofit organization empowering students in developing nations through scholarships, mentorship, and leadership development.

When she's not serving through her finance career or mentoring, you'll find her worshiping, spending time with her family, or deep in honest conversation, usually over something warm.

Connect at: rachel@jathought.org